ANIMALS ATTACK!

Tigers

Nathan Aaseng

KIDHAVEN PRESS

An imprint of Thomson Gale, a part of The Thomson Corporation

THOMSON
™
GALE

Detroit • New York • San Francisco • San Diego • New Haven, Conn. • Waterville, Maine • London • Munich

© 2006 Thomson Gale, a part of The Thomson Corporation.

Thomson and Star Logo are trademarks and Gale and KidHaven Press are registered trademarks used herein under license.

For more information, contact
KidHaven Press
27500 Drake Rd.
Farmington Hills, MI 48331-3535
Or you can visit our Internet site at http://www.gale.com

LIBRARY OF CONGRESS CATALOGING-IN-PUBLICATION DATA

Aaseng, Nathan.
  Tigers / [by Nathan Aaseng].
    p. cm. — (Animals attack)
  Includes bibliographical references.
  Contents: The most dangerous predator—Attacks in the wild—
Never tamed—Protection from tigers.
  ISBN 0-7377-1545-6 (hard cover : alk. paper)
  1. Tigers—Juvenile literature. 2. Tiger attacks—Juvenile literature.
I. Title. II. Series.
  QL737.C23.A155 2005
  599.756—dc22
                                             2005009439

Printed in the United States of America

Contents

Chapter 1

The Most Dangerous Predator

The lion is known as king of the beasts. It is the tiger, however, that is by far the most dangerous and feared cat in the world. In the words of Dutch scholar Peter Boomgaard, "The historical record overwhelmingly favors the view that the tiger was mankind's most [determined] enemy."[1]

Tiger Toll

No one knows exactly how many people tigers have killed over the centuries. Today, tigers are believed to kill between 100 and 300 people each year. This number is especially eye-opening considering how

With its sharp fangs bared, this Siberian tiger shows why these big cats are among the world's most feared animals.

few tigers are left in the wild. While more than 100,000 tigers roamed the jungles of Asia in the early 1900s, their numbers have dwindled to between 5,000 and 7,000 today. Three of the eight **subspecies** of tigers have gone extinct in the past century.

Why Tigers Are Dangerous

Tigers are among the most gifted hunters on Earth. They are the largest of the great cats. Siberian tigers can grow to as large as 13 feet (4m) in length and weigh as much as 750 pounds (340kg). Even the more common Bengal tiger commonly tips the scales at 500 pounds (227kg). Their strength allows them to kill and drag oxen that weigh a ton (0.91 metric ton) over great distances. With sharp claws, large teeth, and strong jaws, they can kill with a single bite to the neck or a swipe of a paw.

In addition to having size and strength, tigers are expert stalkers. Walking on soft pads, they make no sound. Their stripes make them almost impossible to see when they crouch in the shadows of the jungle. After creeping within striking distance, they attack with lightning speed. Tigers can leap 30 feet (9m) in a single bound and can dash at speeds of up to 35 miles per hour (56kph) over a short distance to chase down **prey**.

Humans who walk through tiger territory are easy prey for these superb hunters. Only 1 out of 100 victims of an attack by a man-eating tiger sur-

Built for Attack!

Adult Bengal tigers weigh about 500 pounds and are very strong. They can drag pray over many miles.

The tiger's stripes help it blend into the jungle, allowing it to attack by surprise.

With their sharp teeth and strong jaws, tigers can kill with one bite to the neck.

Soft paw pads allow tigers to stalk prey without making a sound.

Tigers can leap 30 feet in a single bound and can run up to 35 miles per hour.

vives. Few ever see the tiger until it is on them, and they cannot begin to match its strength and quickness. In fact, according to tiger expert John Seidensticker, given all the tiger's advantages, "it is puzzling why they didn't kill more than they did."[2]

Why Tigers Attack

The tiger's diet seldom includes humans. One study of a tiger population showed that only 3 percent of them actively went after human prey.

One reason a tiger might attack is if a person surprises a mother with her cubs. Anyone who approaches an area where cubs are being raised runs a strong risk of attack. As with most wild animals, female tigers will aggressively defend their young from anything they view as a threat.

Another common reason for attacks is hunger. Tigers most likely to stalk and attack humans as

Protective by nature, female tigers will attack anything that comes too close to their cubs.

prey are those that cannot survive on their usual food sources. Unlike lions or wolves, tigers live and hunt alone. Each tiger must be fit enough to bring down prey. Old, sick, or badly injured tigers, and those that have lost teeth, often have trouble bringing down their usual prey. Their only hope of survival may be to go after easier targets. Similarly, tigers that have been chased out of their territory by younger and stronger tigers may be driven by hunger to attack humans.

Most often humans create the conditions that push tigers into resorting to human prey. Millions of people living in Asia move into areas that have been home to tigers for centuries. By cutting down forests for timber or clearing land for farming and raising livestock, they destroy the tiger's natural environment. This **habitat** destruction drives out the animals on which tigers normally feed. With their main food sources gone, tigers become desperate. When a hungry tiger comes across a careless or unwary human, the tiger attacks.

Once they begin targeting humans, tigers become extremely dangerous. Indian wildlife expert Laxoni Mandanthar says, "Our experience is that once a tiger gets a taste of human flesh, it will not eat other animals."[3]

Where Tigers Attack

Most tiger attacks occur in three areas. The most dangerous place is a swamp region in the Ganges

Delta known as the Sundarbans, along the border of India and Bangladesh. The Sundarbans is a huge **mangrove** swamp. Mangroves are trees that grow in the salty water where a river blends into the ocean. Because the water is undrinkable for humans, people do not live in the Sundarbans. The tree roots also make passage by boat difficult, and the water makes travel on land difficult, too. This means that tigers are safe from humans–for the most part.

Many people, however, live just outside the Sundarbans. Most of them are poor. In order to survive they often go into the edges of the Sundarbans to fish, cut wood, or gather honey. About 35,000 people travel into the area each year. When they do, they risk meeting the largest and most dangerous population of tigers on Earth. This is the only place where tigers regularly attack and eat humans even though other prey is available to them. Official records show that roughly 45 people are killed each year by tigers in the Sundarbans, but experts estimate that the number may be as high as 300. A study of 427 deaths from tiger attacks between 1984 and 2001 showed that 53 percent of those killed were fishermen, 15 percent were woodcutters, and 13 percent were honey gatherers. The tigers usually attack in the early morning, late afternoon, or in the hour before midnight.

Other Danger Zones

A second dangerous tiger zone is Royal Chitwan National Park in Nepal, about 150 miles (250km) south-

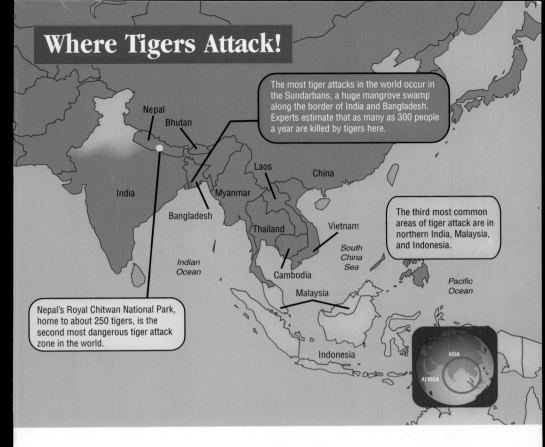

Where Tigers Attack!

Nepal

Bhutan

The most tiger attacks in the world occur in the Sundarbans, a huge mangrove swamp along the border of India and Bangladesh. Experts estimate that as many as 300 people a year are killed by tigers here.

Laos

China

India

Myanmar

Bangladesh

Thailand

Vietnam

The third most common areas of tiger attack are in northern India, Malaysia, and Indonesia.

South China Sea

Indian Ocean

Cambodia

Malaysia

Pacific Ocean

Nepal's Royal Chitwan National Park, home to about 250 tigers, is the second most dangerous tiger attack zone in the world.

Indonesia

ASIA

AFRICA

west of Nepal's capital city of Kathmandu. This relatively new park, the largest in Nepal, is home to some 250 tigers. Unfortunately, the human population around Chitwan has grown rapidly to more than 300,000. The crowding of people into areas where tigers live has created a dangerous situation. In 2001, tigers killed at least nineteen people near Chitwan.

The third most common area of tiger attacks is near tiger habitats that have been destroyed. Tigers whose habitat has been ruined in northern India, Malaysia, and Indonesia wander into settled areas in search of prey. Sugar fields are especially attractive to the tigers. They often follow prey animals

A visitor to a Chinese zoo screams as a captive Siberian tiger lets out a powerful roar.

into the fields. Because the fields require little human care for most of the year, the tigers believe them to be free from humans, and they settle there. When people return to the fields at harvest-time, trouble erupts.

In all three areas of common tiger attacks, the tigers are not looking for humans to attack but are finding more humans wandering into their hunting zones.

Tiger Attacks in Captivity

The tiger's beauty, grace, and power, make it a popular attraction at zoos, wildlife preserves, and even among private pet owners. While tiger populations struggle to survive in the wild, the number of captive tigers has been rapidly growing. A tiger cub can be bought on the Internet for as little as $300. Owning a tiger is legal in 30 of the 50 states. With the booming trade in private tiger sales, nearly twice as many tigers live in captivity than in the wild.

Most tiger attacks in captivity occur when people are careless or foolish enough to provoke a tiger. Others occur simply because tigers are dangerous. Even a playful tiger can accidentally cause great harm. Whether entering a tiger habitat or a tiger cage, people need to be on their guard. In either place, there is no guarantee that a tiger will not attack.

Attacks in the Wild

During the early 20th century, man-eating tigers terrorized villages in India. So stealthy and deadly were these beasts that the people could do nothing to prevent the attacks.

The tigers of the Sundarbans are perhaps the most mysterious of the man-eating tigers. Unlike the Champawat tiger and other man-eaters, they do not focus on only human prey. If they did, they would have to kill 24,000 people a year. Yet they clearly include the occasional human among their prey.

Sundarbans tigers have been observed to single out a human from a group of workers. They may stalk that person for many hours as they seek the best opportunity to attack.

One of the most deadly of these cats was believed to have killed 52 people between 1989 and 1994. Its victims never saw it coming. Relying on its stripes to hide amid the dark and shadowy forest, the tiger crept close and then pounced from behind. In typical tiger fashion, it grabbed its victim by the back of the neck, crushing the spinal cord, or bit the throat. Either method caused instant death.

The Sundarbans tigers are fairly safe from human hunters. They can retreat back into the impassable

How Big Is a Tiger?

6 feet			
5 feet			
4 feet			
3 feet			
2 feet			
1 foot			
	Man 200 lbs.	Teenage girl 115 lbs.	Bengal tiger 500 lbs.

This Bengal tiger buries its long fangs into a deer carcass and drags off the prey with its powerful jaws.

watery darkness of the mangrove swamp. The man-eater of the early 1990s likely would have gone on killing for months were it not for a freak accident. It had singled out and stalked its latest victim, a wood-cutter. As the tiger attacked, the woodcutter sped off in a panic. According to forest officer Maharraf Hossain,

"The tiger chased him and he [the woodcutter] stumbled along the ground along with his axe, which sliced the forehead of the tiger."[4]

Recently, a tiger may have far surpassed that tiger's record of victims in the Sundarbans. As of June 2004, it had been blamed for as many as 159 deaths. According to tracker Khasru Chowdhury, "It is possible that there are two man-eaters in the forests. But so far I have evidence suggesting there is one crazy male tiger of medium size, who has been preying on humans since 2002."[5]

Attacks upon the Water

One of the most common mistakes people make about tigers is thinking they are strictly land animals. A person sitting in a boat in open water would appear

From its hiding spot in the grass growing along a lakeshore, a Siberian tiger leaps at its prey.

to be safe from attack. Tigers, however, are excellent swimmers and show no fear of going into the water to attack people. The majority of people killed by tigers in the Sundarbans, in fact, have been fishermen. Such people are especially at risk because they sit out in the open—where they can be easily seen—for hours at a time.

Recently, a man named Sarnder was fishing from a boat with friends on one of the waterways in the Sundarbans. As the sun was setting, the men began pulling in their nets. Before any of them

A fisherman shows the deep scars on his head from a vicious tiger attack in the Sundarbans.

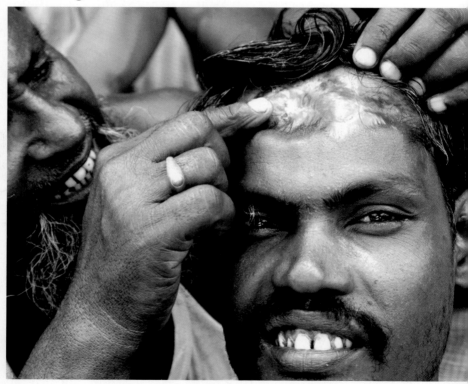

could react, a tiger exploded out of the jungle and leapt toward the boat. It grabbed Sarnder by the back of the neck and dragged him out of the boat, through the water and into the forest. The man was not seen again.

It was not that he and his family were unaware of the danger. However, as Sarnder's wife explained after his death, "If my husband didn't go out on the river, we wouldn't survive."[6]

Villagers in the area report that even fishermen on larger boats have fallen victim to tigers. One tiger swam to a boat and climbed onto the deck. It killed one of the sleeping crewmen and carried him back into the jungle.

Tigers are known to attack on the water in other parts of India as well. Joy Kumar Modal, a crab fishermen, was one of the lucky ones. He was fishing for crabs with three others near the Annpur Hamlet when a tiger charged from the woods. The beast swam to them, climbed into their canoe, and attacked Modal. Fortunately his father was able to shove the tiger back into the water before it could deal a fatal blow. Modal escaped with three claw wounds.

Driven to Attack

Until recently, tiger attacks were rare in Malaysia and Indonesia. Illegal logging, which has destroyed millions of acres (hectares) of rain forest, has changed this. This activity has created a dangerous situation in these lands.

In November 18, 2003, four professional timber thieves finished a long day of cutting rain-forest trees with their chain saws near Pelindang, Indonesia. As darkness fell, three of them rested atop a raised wooden platform, where the group slept to keep them safe from tiger attacks at night. Below them, 23-year-old Siadul was preparing supper.

Without warning, a Sumatran tiger charged from the darkness. It bit a large chunk from Siadul and began to drag him away. "It was like a cat catching a rat,"[7] said one of his shaken friends. The tiger would have gotten away with its meal, but Siadul's body became stuck on a log. His friends started their chain saws and scared the tiger away. Siadul did not survive.

A Dumai forest policeman explained the reason for the attack: "Most of the tigers we catch are thin. I think it is because they cannot find their usual food. They go into the villages and eat whatever they can find."[8]

Desperate Tigers

Starving tigers will take actions that no well-fed tiger would try. On the night of April 2, 1999, a young tigress living in Royal Chitwan Park walked boldly into the nearby village of Syanlibas. It stopped at an empty house where it could smell meat left by the owners. Frustrated at not being able to break into the place, it went to another house. There it found 69-year-old Sheta Kumari Pant and her husband

This starving tiger is desperate for food and will attack most anything in its path.

sleeping on the porch. The tiger dragged the woman around the back of the building and began to eat. The husband returned with friends to drive the tiger away, but the woman was dead.

The next night, the tiger returned to the village and entered another building. There, it attacked and killed 35-year-old Devi Adhikari. When the tiger was caught shortly after, it was obvious that the beast had been starving.

Because they are stealthy, lone hunters, tigers may lurk unseen just about anywhere within their range. Many of them will not pass up a chance to attack easy prey, whether human or another animal. Tigers that are unable to find or catch their normal prey are far more likely to look for humans to attack.

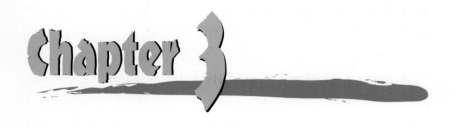

Never Tamed

Since 1990, dozens of people have been killed and several hundred badly injured by tigers in captivity. In the United States alone, captive tigers kill an average of two people each year. Most of these tragedies could have been prevented if people heeded the simple advice of Richard Lattis, director of the Bronx Zoo: "No matter how tame a tiger might seem, it isn't tame."[9]

Pet Tigers and Children: A Dangerous Mix

Children are often careless around tigers. On March 15, 2000, four-year-old Jason was visiting the home

Although this captive tiger may appear tame, at any moment she could attack the woman petting her.

of his aunt and uncle, Nancy and Larry Tidwell, in Channelview, Texas. No one was paying attention as Jason wandered into the backyard. There he found the Tidwells' 400-pound pet Bengal tiger (181-kg), Cheyenne, in its 15-by-18-foot cage (4.5m by 5.5m). The family had raised the tiger since it was seven days old. They considered it so tame, they swam with it in their pool.

The curious youngster stuck his hand through the chain-link fence. An instant later, his screams brought the adults running. Cheyenne had bitten off the boy's right arm above the elbow. As Brian Werner of the Missing Link Foundation explained, "Anything that goes into a tiger's cage, it regards as either a toy or food."[10]

Jason was rushed to Memorial Children's Hospital in nearby Houston, where his arm was reattached in a nine-hour operation. Although he recovered from the attack, Jason faced more surgery and years of rehabilitation to regain the use of the arm.

One of the neighbors was shocked by the incident. "The tiger is very passive," she said. "I've let my daughter feed it, and it licked her face."[11]

Even when playing, this captive tiger presents a serious danger to his handler, a Thai Buddhist monk.

"A Time Bomb Waiting to Go Off"

Tigers are most content roaming in large sections of wilderness, where they can be by themselves. Experts such as Nicole Paquett of the Animal Protection Institute believe that the tamest of tigers are under severe stress in any sort of enclosure. A tiger under stress, says Paquett, "is a time bomb waiting to go off."[12] It is impossible to say what will trigger the explosion.

On September 20, 2002, a tiger trainer was leading a young tiger out of the Baymonte Christian School auditorium in Scotts Valley, California, at the end of a show. The tiger had never shown any hostility toward anyone. When some kids jumped out of their seats, however, the tiger came to life. It broke free from the trainer, jumped over rows of chairs, and clamped its jaws over the head of a kindergartner. The principal was able to pull the tiger off before it did serious damage.

On November 21, 2004, veteran tiger handler Curt LoGiudice brought a tiger to a Florida county fair. At the end of the day, he was leading the animal away when a fourteen-year-old boy approached and made a sudden move. The tiger attacked and pushed the boy to the ground. When LoGiudice jumped in to save the boy, the tiger began to bite and claw him. The animal was stopped by stun guns before the attack turned deadly.

Clayton James Eller was not so fortunate. On December 15, 2003, he was shoveling snow at his

This Siberian tiger in a Florida zoo later killed one of its handlers as he was repairing its cage.

aunt's home in Miller Creek, North Carolina. The sidewalk ran past the cage of his aunt's pet tiger. Suddenly the tiger reached through an opening at the bottom of the fence and pulled the ten-year-old into the cage. Eller's uncle heard the screams, ran for his gun, and shot the tiger. It was too late to save Eller.

Attack at the Mirage Hotel

If anyone could claim to have tamed tigers it was Roy Horn. The famous Las Vegas showman had demonstrated an amazing ability to communicate with the big cats. He trained his white tigers through

Famed Las Vegas entertainers Siegfried and Roy pose with Montecore and several white tiger cubs.

affection conditioning. This means Horn took care of the cubs from the time they were born and slept with them until they were a year old. This helped him gain the animals' trust. His method appeared to be foolproof. In 30,000 shows with his partner, Siegfried, there had never been an injury of any kind.

On October 3, 2003, Horn was feeling especially good after celebrating his 59th birthday. A crowd of 1,500 showed up for the show at the Mirage Hotel. All went according to routine during the first 45 minutes. Then Horn brought out Montecore, a 380-pound (172kg) seven-year-old white tiger.

Montecore Attacks

Apparently someone in the crowd did something to distract the tiger. Instead of going through his routine, Montecore walked toward the edge of the stage. With no barrier between the tiger and the audience just a few feet (meters) away, the situation suddenly grew alarming. Horn quickly placed himself between the tiger and the audience and ordered Montecore to lie down. The tiger paid no attention and moved closer to the audience.

Horn repeated his commands more urgently. The tiger grabbed Horn's right wrist with his paw. Horn hit the tiger on the head with his wireless microphone, crying, "Release."

When the tiger finally let go, the move caught Horn off balance. The trainer fell backward and tripped over the tiger's leg. When Horn hit the floor, Montecore pounced and bit down on Horn's neck.

Siegfried raced onto the stage, screaming at the tiger to stop. Montecore did not stop. In the words of one audience witness, "He just grabbed him by the throat and walked off stage."[13]

One of the show workers sprayed the tiger with a fire extinguisher, but the cat would not release Horn. Finally the man smacked the tiger on the head with the extinguisher. Montecore let go of Horn and retreated to his cage.

Bleeding from deep wounds to the neck, Horn pleaded that no one harm the tiger. He was rushed to a trauma center, where he immediately went into surgery. Few expected Horn would live through the night. The next morning he suffered a stroke and had to undergo more surgery. The attack left him with a crushed windpipe, unable to speak or swallow, and with a paralyzed left side.

Horn gradually improved, but it was not until mid-November that he could breathe on his own. He then faced many health problems and more surgeries.

What Went Wrong

Horn's partner claimed that Montecore's attack was not really an attack. He insisted that Horn was having a bad reaction to some blood pressure pills and was not feeling well. Montecore realized that something

During each performance, Horn placed himself in very dangerous situations with his white tigers.

was wrong with his master and tried to protect him. The tiger simply did not realize that in pulling Horn to safety, he was actually killing him.

Other animal experts disagreed. "The cat wasn't trying to protect him," argued Jonathan Kraft of Keepers of the Wild. "That was a typical killing bite."[14] To these experts, the mystery was not why Montecore attacked, but how Siegfried and Horn had managed to go so long without such an attack. They viewed the episode as a reminder that tigers, even the most tame ones, are wild. "Even though they're raised in captivity and they love us, sometimes their natural instincts just take over,"[15] said one trainer.

Chapter 4

Protection from Tigers

Protection from tigers in captivity is almost completely a matter of taking proper safety precautions. Tiger attacks in the wild are a different story. Not too long ago, many people believed that the only solution to tiger attacks in the wild was simply to kill the tigers or remove them to zoos.

Most problems between tigers and humans are the result of humans moving into tiger territory and destroying their habitat. The simplest way to avoid tiger attacks is for people to stay out of tiger territory. As one Indian remarked after a villager had been killed by a tiger while gathering wood in the forest, "If the tiger had come to our home and killed us it

A Sumatran tiger in an Autralian zoo warns onlookers to keep their distance.

would be appropriate to kill the tiger, but since that's not the case, it would not be appropriate."[16]

There are two ways to keep people away from wild tigers. One is to restrict travel in known tiger habitats. Increased supervision of those entering the Sundarbans was credited with reducing the amount of tiger attacks in the later 1990s. Especially important was a rule that bans people from collecting **phoenix palm** fronds to use in thatching their houses. Female tigers like to live among these palms when raising their cubs.

A second way to keep people away from tigers is to create and maintain **buffer zones** between human populations and tiger habitats. A buffer zone is an area where neither tigers nor humans go

Tourists at a game reserve in India watch from a safe distance as a Bengal tiger crosses the road.

Preserving the habitat of tigers and their prey helps prevent attacks on humans.

on a regular basis. Such a zone was originally created at Royal Chitwan Park, and it worked well. When the exploding human population moved into the zone, however, problems began.

In other areas, humans have destroyed not only buffer zones but the habitat in which tigers live. Illegal logging in rain forests and the clearing of land for crops rob tigers of the wilderness area they need to survive. Along with illegal hunting, it also reduces the number of prey animals. Tigers with no place to roam and hunt, and little prey to eat, must search for new territory: While on the move, they run into humans. The hungrier they get, the more likely they are to attack and eat them.

Experts believe that preserving natural habitats is the single most important step people can take to protect human populations from tiger attacks. As one says, "Tigers living in a healthy jungle don't have to eat people."[17]

Masks and Dummies

Tiger protection in the Sundarbans has been difficult. The tigers there live in a healthy, isolated habitat. Yet they continue to attack humans who enter their domain for brief periods of time. Many of the people who live on the edge of the Sundarbans could not survive without fishing, logging, and gathering honey in the swamp.

The government has begun an effort to provide work for people that would keep them out of the Sundarbans. The most promising of these is the establishment of a shrimp farming business in the saltwater marshes.

While such efforts hold the greatest hope for reducing tiger attacks in the area, it will take years before they have an impact. Meanwhile, many creative plans have been designed to protect people from tigers in the Sundarbans. After noticing that tigers almost always attack from behind, the government began issuing rubber face masks in 1986. The masks were to be worn on the back of the head. The plan was a tremendous success at first. Over the next year, 2,500 workers visiting the area wore masks. Not one was attacked. Meanwhile, 30 workers who did not wear the masks were killed. Tigers were observed following masked workers for up to eight hours but never attacked.

Over time, however, tigers appeared to catch on to the trick. After the initial success in the late 1980s, attacks rose again in the next decade. The government has been undecided on the masks' effectiveness. After abandoning the idea for several years, it has now reintroduced the masks on a large scale.

The government also has tried to discourage tiger attacks through **shock conditioning**. They do this by dressing up clay dummies in outfits worn by honey gatherers or fishermen. The dummies are soaked with urine to give them a strong human scent and placed in the mangrove swamp. When a tiger attacks a dummy, it is hit with a 300-volt electrical shock. The hope is that the shocks will discourage tigers from attacking anyone similarly dressed.

Water, Pigs, Clubs, and Shrimp

Some researchers have suggested that the salty water of the swamp affects the tigers, making them more ag-

These woodcutters in the Sundarbans wear masks on the back of their heads to confuse tigers, which typically attack from behind.

gressive. They have brought freshwater into the area for tigers to drink, but no one has noticed any improvement in tiger attitudes.

Others have tried to glut the Sundarbans with prey so that the tigers will not bother with humans.

Because tigers are deadly creatures that prey on other animals, people sharing the tiger's world must take great care to avoid attacks.

To this end, pigs have been bred and released into the tiger domain. Again, no noticeable results have been seen.

Tigers are unpredictable and adaptable creatures. There is no way to guarantee safety when entering the tiger's domain. Tigers are wild, dangerous creatures. While many steps can be taken to keep humans out of their reach, people will always have to exercise extreme care when sharing the tiger's world.

Notes

Chapter 1: The Most Dangerous Predator

1. Quoted in Jim Doherty, "Tigers at the Gate," *Smithsonian,* January 2002, p. 66.
2. Quoted in Adele Conover, "The Object at Hand," *Smithsonian,* November 1995. www.smithsonianmag.com/smithsonian/issues95/nov95/object_nov95.html.
3. Quoted in Keshab Poudel, "Man-Eating Tigers Kill 16 Nepalese in Two Months," *One World South Asia,* April 1, 2004. www.oneworld.net/article/view/82906/1.

Chapter 2: Attacks in the Wild

4. Quoted in Sharier Khan, "Man-Eating Tigers Terrorize Bangladesh Forests," *One World South Asia.* www.oneworld.net/article/view/82906/1.
5. Quoted in Khan, "Man-Eating Tigers Terrorize Bangladesh Forests."
6. Quoted in Miriam Jordan, "Safety from Man-Eaters," *Christian Science Monitor,* February 25, 1998. http://csmonitor.com/cgi-bin/durableRedirect.pl?/durable/1998/02/25/intl/intl.1.html.
7. Quoted in Richard C. Paddock, "Unkindest Cuts Scar Indonesia," *Los Angeles Times,* January 2, 2004.

www.mongabay.com/external/tigers_indo_2004.
htm.

8. Quoted in Paddock, "Unkindest Cuts Scar Indonesia."

Chapter 3: Never Tamed

9. Quoted in Michael Lemmick, "Never Trust a Tiger," *Time,* October 20, 2003, p.13.
10. Quoted in Alex Tresniewski, "Racing the Clock," *People Weekly,* April 3, 2000, p. 85.
11. Quoted in Tresniewski, "Racing the Clock," p. 85.
12. Quoted in Lemmick, "Never Trust a Tiger," p. 14.
13. Quoted in Alana Nash, "Stage Fright: What Really Happened," *Reader's Digest,* April 2004, p. 138.
14. Quoted in Steve Crupi, "Experts: Tiger Wasn't Trying to Protect Roy," *WorldNow,* October 10, 2003. www.kvbc.com/Global/story.asp?S=1477 353&nav=15MUCBSd.
15. Quoted in Nash, "Stage Fright," p. 139.

Chapter 4: Protection from Tigers

16. Quoted in Doherty, "Tigers at the Gate," p. 66.
17. John Seidensticker, "Tiger Tracks," *Smithsonian,* January 2002, p. 62.

Glossary

affection conditioning: Animal training technique in which a trainer goes to great lengths to care for and have personal contact with the animal in order to gain its trust.

buffer zones: Areas that separate two or more populations that might be in conflict with each other if they were in direct contact.

habitat: The natural surroundings in which an animal lives.

mangrove: A unique kind of tree noted for its tangled surface roots that grows well in wet, salty environments.

phoenix palm: A tropical tree that grows large, feathery leaves.

prey: The animals that a predator such as a tiger prefers to eat.

shock conditioning: A method of training that teaches animals to avoid certain things through the use of electrical shocks.

subspecies: A group of animals that have many similar features that separate them even from other animals to whom they are closely related.

For Further Exploration

Books

Maurice Hornocker, *Track of the Tiger*. San Francisco: Sierra Club, 1997. A very readable book with 75 beautiful photographs of tigers in the wild.

John Seidensticker, *Tigers (World Life Library)*. Stillwater, MN: 1996. One of the world's tiger experts covers all the basic facts and includes 50 pictures.

Vivek Sinha, *The Vanishing Tiger: Wild Tigers, Copredators, and Prey Species*. London: Salamander Press, 2003. For stronger readers, this book is a well-photographed account of a trip into the habitat of Indian tigers. Information on photographing tigers is included.

Web Sites

Big Cat Rescue (www.bigcatrescue.org). This Web site, run by a nonprofit educational organization concerned with preserving tigers, is packed with information, including a listing and description of literally hundreds of big cat attacks.

Cat Specialist Group (http://lynx.uio.no/cat folk/mjissues/mjchp_21.htm). This Web site provides a very thorough look at many of the issues that threaten tigers. Chapter 2 is of particular interest, as it provides a study of tiger-to-human conflicts over the years and suggests ways to ease the problems.

5Tigers (www.5tigers.org). An information-packed Web site that includes news, facts about tigers, and interactive experiences (such as tracking and identifying an escaped tiger).

Index

Picture Credits

About the Author

Nathan Aaseng has written more than 170 books, many of them for young readers. He majored in biology and English at Luther College in Iowa.